A Covenant in Wonder with the World

The Power of Stories and Songs

A Covenant in Wonder with the World

The Power of Stories and Songs

THE 2010 GRAND RIVER FORUM LECTURE

WILFRID LAURIER UNIVERSITY BRANTFORD CAMPUS

J. Edward Chamberlin

RONSDALE PRESS

VANCOUVER

A COVENANT IN WONDER WITH THE WORLD
Copyright © 2012 J. Edward Chamberlin

Ronsdale Press
3350 West 21st Avenue
Vancouver, B.C., Canada
V6S 1G7

Set in Minion: 11 on 15
Typesetting: Julie Cochrane
Printing: Island Blue, Victoria, B.C., Canada
Cover Design: Mouki K. Butt & Deirdre Salisbury
Front Cover Photo: The Lakota Sioux Horse Effigy (Courtesy of Museum of
    South Dakota State Historical Society)
Back Cover Photo: J. Edward Chamberlin: |Una Rooi of the ╪Khomani people

Ronsdale Press wishes to thank the following for their support of its publishing
program: the Canada Council for the Arts, the Government of Canada through the
Canada Book Fund, the British Columbia Arts Council, and the Province of British
Columbia through the British Columbia Book Publishing Tax Credit program.

LIBRARY AND ARCHIVES CANADA CATALOGUING IN PUBLICATION

Chamberlin, J. Edward, 1943–
    A covenant in wonder with the world: the power of stories and songs /
J. Edward Chamberlin.

The Grand River Forum lecture, delivered at Wilfrid Laurier's
    Brantford campus.
Issued also in electronic format.
ISBN 978-1-55380-148-1

    1. Fiction. 2. Poetry. 3. Oral tradition. 4. Sacred space in literature.
I. Title.

PN3338.C43 2011   808.3   C2011-906643-2

ACKNOWLEDGEMENTS

First of all, my thanks to Professor Ian MacRae of Laurier Brantford for his generous hospitality, his inspiring leadership, and his commitment to putting questions before answers. I am deeply grateful to him and his colleagues, and honoured to have been part of this first Grand River Forum. Some elements of this talk were first tried out in Toronto in March 2010, as the Larkin–Stuart Lectures, co-sponsored by Trinity College and St. Thomas's Anglican Church. I thank Provost Andy Orchard and Rev. Mark Andrews for their kind invitation, and the audience for its genial response. A couple of the stories that I tell here have also appeared in other places, but I hope the occasion of this Grand River Forum refreshes them.

INTRODUCTION

It is a pleasure and a privilege to introduce J. Edward Chamberlin to you as the first annual Grand River Forum Lecturer at Wilfrid Laurier University's Brantford campus. Laurier Brantford is home to the largest undergraduate core program in Canada — Contemporary Studies (CT). CT courses are designed to address the complexity of contemporary issues — in ethics, the environment, citizenship and social justice — from multiple perspectives in the humanities and social sciences. All students at Laurier Brantford enroll in Contemporary Studies, with many doing a joint major in another program. This situation creates some genuine possibilities, one of which is a still-new initiative, the Grand River Forum, in which all incoming Brantford students are assigned to read a common text in the summer before their first year. The chosen book should combine good writing (accessible, for a non-specialist audience) with substantive interdisciplinary concerns. Each year a new text, and a new series of issues, will be addressed — ideally from a different disciplinary perspective, and with a different faculty member at the helm. The Grand River Forum is meant to emphasize dialogue, discussion, and a larger campus conversation, so that when students move into residence and meet their mates for the first time, they will already share a common text, and perhaps many opinions about it.

Laurier Brantford's Development Team, Vice President of Student Affairs David McMurray, Brantford Dean Bruce Arai, President Max Blouw, and the Contemporary Studies program have been instrumental in supporting this program. They see the Grand River Forum as a way to strengthen the core curriculum at Laurier Brantford, and of furthering the interdisciplinary conversation among students, faculty, and the wider world. This is the conversation around which Laurier Brantford was founded, and for some time now has been based.

The 2010 Forum text was J. Edward Chamberlin's *If This Is Your Land, Where Are Your Stories? Finding Common Ground* (2003). Over six hundred members of the Laurier Brantford community read this book. Some dove straight in; others may still be puzzling over its many meanings. In his University Lecture, Dr. Chamberlin sheds new light on some of the old contradictions, wonders, and tensions his writing brings up — the ceremonies of belief that give currency and credit to our covenants, constitutions, and creation stories, and to our various traditions in science and the arts, in liturgy and law. He treats the strange power of stories and songs to bring people together, and to pull us apart. There is a long history of both types of story along the banks of the Grand.

The centrepiece of the Forum is that the book's author visits campus for a few days in the fall to participate in meetings and lectures with students and faculty. A number of first-year Contemporary Studies courses incorporated the book as a required text; a fourth year Special Topics course was organized around the text and its themes; a range of other courses and programs adopted the book. An Artists Speak! series was held, in which students worked with local artists and the Brantford Arts Block to produce individual and collective visual responses to the themes of the forum. The collective piece mapped the "deep history" of life on the Grand River, documenting the collision and commingling of cultures and histories that might well constitute Brantford's common ground. The Forum Conference, in which faculty and student presenters treated a shared set of themes in a genuinely interdisciplinary manner, created a dialogue among diverse research programs that frankly startled us in its clarity and conviction. A forthcoming issue of the *Journal of Canadian Studies* has evolved from this day. Not least, an Arts Opening and reception was held, with student artmakers guiding us through their works. Dr. Chamberlin's conference keynote address was titled "'If You Are Ignorant, Books Cannot Laugh at You': The Value of an

Interdisciplinary Core Curriculum." Both of his lectures are video archived at Vimeo and Fora.tv.

Dr. Chamberlin has lectured widely around the world on cultural and political issues, on literature and the arts. A university professor emeritus in English and Comparative Literature at the University of Toronto, an Oxford-educated scholar from the tall-grass prairies of Alberta by way of the mountainous interior of B.C., a river-running canoeist and hunting guide with degrees in mathematics and English, Dr. Chamberlin has worked for over thirty years on land claims in Canada, the United States, Africa and Australia. Some of these stories from the field surface in his work, in which he characteristically moves from traveller's tales to linguistic theory, from cowboy poetry to supreme court verdicts, from raging sixteenth-century debates that haunt us still, to bedtime stories and nursery rhymes. Only in his work have I found a U2 song referred to as a prayer, Rastafarianism celebrated as a great creation story of the Americas, and the old dichotomy of civilization versus barbarism seen from a thousand angles, like a cubist painting that always manages to just cohere.

Dr. Chamberlin has written books on Oscar Wilde, *Ripe was the Drowsy Hour* (1977), on native and non-native relations in Canada, *The Harrowing of Eden* (1975), and on horses, *Horse* (2006), those wonderfully powerful and purposeful creatures he calls both a necessity and a luxury. His book on West Indian poetry, *Come Back to Me My Language* (1993), is a foundational text in the field. Further still, Dr. Chamberlin is former poetry editor of *Saturday Night* magazine, and senior research associate with the Royal Commission on Aboriginal Peoples in Canada. It is a great blessing that he has been able to join us at Laurier Brantford, where contradictory claims on the land and the concomitant tensions of civil and uncivil society remain unresolved. Ted Chamberlin has been finding common ground between natives and newcomers for a very long time.

— Ian J. MacRae
Founder & Coordinator Grand River Forum

A COVENANT IN WONDER WITH THE WORLD
THE POWER OF STORIES AND SONGS

In a wonderful book called *Suddenly They Heard Footsteps*, the Toronto storyteller Dan Yashinsky describes the quintessential signature of storytelling at that quintessentially Canadian storytelling ceremony, an evening campfire at a summer camp near Bolton, in Ontario, where he was a counsellor. Another counsellor had just finished telling the tale of Old Man Bolton, a grim and ghostly figure who lived in the neighbourhood long ago — which is to say, before flashlights — and was said to do all sorts of frightening things, a number of which the storyteller had just described . . . things likely to strike fear into the heart of anyone out there in the woods, especially now that the campfire was dying out and dark had settled down.

He finished the story, and after a pause designed to heighten the wonder — and the dread — of it all, said cheerfully "bed-time, kids. Off to your tents." Nobody moved. "Bed-time," he repeated. Still nobody moved. Finally, a still, small voice spoke up. "Is old man Bolton still alive?" "Probably not," said the counsellor.

That "probably not" is at the heart of all stories. So, of course, is "probably." Every story, in every society, hovers — or shuttles — between them, with allegiances to both. "We're not sure" is the signature of good science, even as "we are sure" is the signature of its storytelling. In the arts, it's often the other way around. The Danish writer Jens Peter Jacobsen — whose work inspired artists as different as the poet Rainer Maria Rilke, the composer Arnold Schoenberg, and the painter Paul Klee — once wrote a short story that he called "Two Worlds" . . . but he said that if the language had allowed he would have called it "Two World." That's the world of stories, the world of both probably and probably not; and in a correspondence acknowledged across cultures, such stories make the world — or the two world — we live in. Or some say it is the archetypal trickster, the storyteller rather than the story, who does so, striking a deal that goes to the heart of what it is to be human.

Humans are hard-wired for making deals, which is to say, hard-wired for belief and for the ceremonies that nourish it. Language may be the earliest of these, which is why it is sometimes said that we are genetically coded for language. But I think it is for belief, and for ceremony — both of which underwrite language — and for the covenants in wonder and the constitutions of community that represent the most important deals we make with ourselves, with others, with what we call reality, and with the mysterious powers around and within us.

Covenants are binding agreements. They often involve the divine, and the language used to describe spiritual powers reminds us of the obligations they impose and the obedience they demand. For many of us, covenants have strong Biblical associations, differently conceived in the Old and the New Testaments, with "testament" itself a translation of the Greek word for covenant. And covenants can have legal as well as religious authority, familiar in land transactions where they effect or restrict ownership. Indeed, restrictive covenants have a long history, and Abraham's deal with his god is merely one of the most famous.

A constitution, on the other hand, has moved in meaning from a point in classical rhetoric — framing a question or an argument — to the nature of the human body and finally to regulation, which is the sense in which it was used by Henry II in England in the middle of the twelfth century to describe his early attempt to turn unwritten custom into statute. Nowadays, constitutions often refer to the whole structure of a society, and to the rights and duties of individuals in relation to the power of the state or the church. Like covenants, constitutions sometimes have an elusive character, nicely illustrated by the way in which England was described in the eighteenth century as the only monarchy in the world with a constitution, and in the nineteenth century as the only democracy without one. Stories and songs that define a community are often said to provide its constitution, and it is this connection that gives a national literature its edge. But the same stories and songs also give a covenantal stamp to collective identity, sealing a deal that both holds communities together and keeps them apart from others.

Language is an important part of both covenants and constitutions, as well as of communities; and whether it begins with words or with phrases, with gestures or with music, language becomes one of the biggest deals we enter into as humans. The association of commerce with language is very old, with words credited in much the way we credit other forms of currency. We believe that words mean something, and are worth something, even though we know they are simply sounds and scripts to which we assign value according to local custom, just as we credit coin and paper currency with value even though it is usually worth nothing in itself. Credit, after all, means he or she believes. We depend for the power of language on a collective belief in its value. Accordingly, deflation or inflation are constant threats, with literary critics and newspaper columnists and writers of letters to the editor maintaining standards like governors of a central bank.

Language also presents us with a contrast, being an agent of both fate and freedom, determining our thoughts and feelings on the one hand and emancipating them on the other. Intelligent people have disagreed about which is more important for a very long time. William Wordsworth and Samuel Taylor Coleridge, who were close friends and collaborators on so many other subjects, took opposite sides. Wordsworth was convinced that language embodied thought (language is its incarnation, was his image, and he described in his poem "Intimations of Immortality from Recollections of Early Childhood" how "shades of the prison-house begin to close upon" us as we grow up and learn a language). Coleridge, on the other hand, believed that language merely conveyed thought (as a slide rule calculates sums, he said, liberating us).

A little earlier, the eighteenth-century scholar Giambattista Vico argued that we misrepresent much of the world because of the structure of our languages, offering an early version of the coding of language (to which feminists brought renewed attention a generation ago) when he contended what a difference it would make if we thought of God as a verb rather than a noun. Whatever side we take — and most of us sit on the fence — language can be both an instrument of confinement and a force for freedom. Both have their appeal. When we are confined or enclosed, we have a strong sense of community — there's no community quite like a prison community — in which every language, even every dialect (as the psychologist Frantz Fanon used to say), is a way of thinking and feeling and behaving. When we are liberated, we can re-create the world in our own image, or at least in the image of our language.

Language, of course, also gives us stories and songs, and they in turn give shape and substance to the things we believe in, from the elegant theories and elaborate explanations of the sciences to the poems and performances of the arts, and from the praise songs of philosophy and politics to the storylines of the professions. They perpetuate ideals and identities, and they provoke controversy and conflict. They include our explanations of the origin and purpose of things, of causes and effects and sequences of events, and of our relationship to the forces that surround us; the institutions we establish, the ways in which we constitute ourselves as communities, and the covenants we enter into with secular as well as spiritual powers. In one way or another, these stories and songs provide both our declaration of independence from the tyranny of the everyday and our first line of defence against it, bringing order to chaos and dignity to the fierce and often fatal indecencies of life. All stories and songs provide a way of managing life and death, the joy and sadness of love, the mysteries of friendship and contentment, and the menace of accidents and disease. That hasn't changed in ten thousand years, for we understand many of these things little better now than we did during the last ice age; and the impulse to turn to stories and songs to push back against the realities of the world is ancient and universal.

The stories and songs by means of which we make sense of the world represent both things as they are or seem to be, and things as we wish they were or wonder whether they might be; both the so-called real world, its reality conditioned by our habits of thought and feeling, and the world of our imaginations, shaped by our anxieties and desires. We try to keep these two worlds in balance — which is, in a way, made easier because there is always tension between them — just as we try to balance the natural and the divine worlds, recognizing their separate domains while acknowledging that we cannot do without either.

Wonder is involved in both worlds. Wonder, and wondering. We cannot choose between them, just as we cannot separate thought and feeling; and if we try to do so, we end up with the kind of amazement that is satisfied with the first explanation, or the kind of curiosity that is incapable of genuine surprise. For, just as wonder is always accompanied by wondering, so belief is always surrounded by doubt. If we are at all engaged with life we wonder about the deals we make, the beliefs we embrace. This wonder takes many forms, incorporating scientific as well as religious inquiry and informing both political and legal arrangements. It also influences the distinctions we make between the human and the divine, the material and the spiritual, the natural and the supernatural. "To remain fully human and humane, we must live as though the more than human matters," says Steven Trimble in an essay titled "Covenant" from a small volume published in Alaska in defence of the Arctic National Wildlife Refuge in Gwich'in territory. In another essay in the same collection, Scott Russell Sanders suggests that the wonder of wilderness, of a natural world that humans do not dominate, "represents in space what the Sabbath represents in time — a limit to our dominion, a refuge from the quest for power and wealth, an acknowledgement that the earth does not belong to us." This is the opposite of Robert Frost's regrettable line (from his poem "The Gift Outright") that "the land was ours before we were the land's," though Frost catches himself a few lines later when he says that we "found salvation in surrender." But more in key with the covenantal character of our

Robert Frost (1874–1963)

relationship to the land is his haunting poem "Stopping by Woods on a Snowy Evening," with its curiously phrased opening line — "Whose woods these are I think I know" — and its concluding turn into the language of deal-making, the quintessential signal of a covenant: "But I have promises to keep."

Most of us recognize that we have obligations to the natural world — promises to keep — and that nature will enforce these promises even if nations will not; and such obligations themselves become another kind of covenant. The word environment was first used in its now familiar ecological sense only a half century ago, but it was given the broader meaning of "everything around us" by Thomas Carlyle a century earlier. Carlyle said a lot of questionable things, but one of his wise coinages came in the form of the phrase "natural supernaturalism." The phrase appealed to revolutionaries and reactionaries alike, and it helped give credit to the idea that the imagined world is the only world that matters because it is the only world we know. Science and religion have always understood this, and it is the burden of Oscar Wilde's comment (in his mischievously titled essay "The Decay of Lying") that "life imitates art." It also informs the belief, both ancient and modern, that (in the words of Psalm 90) we live our life as "a tale that is told."

Both worlds — the real and the imagined, the natural and the supernatural — are governed by laws, which to have any force must be underwritten by custom or habit. The rule of law, like the rule of deal-making, is universal, though specific laws and the deals they sponsor vary from place to place and from time to time. Some of them are vicious, as the blood-soaked deity treading the grapes of wrath in the Old Testament and Tennyson's nature "red in tooth and claw" remind us; and we have plenty of evidence of brutal human legislation. And then there are the laws that we deem to have been decreed by divine ordinance. All of them, secular or sacred, are in some sense customary, and involve a surrender to ceremonies within which decrees and decisions must be acknowledged. Believe them, or not . . . but if not, then you are out of the deal, outside the covenant, an outlaw. So most of us believe in such laws, of at least in the idea of them. We believe them, and not.

Stories and songs — to which we give the fancier name literature — teach us to believe the unbelievable, what Coleridge (referring to Plato) called "dear gorgeous nonsense." Metaphors — where things are something that they obviously (for the metaphor to work) are not — routinely present us with this nonsense. And poems often challenge us right from the start. "I saw Eternity the other night," said the great seventeenth-century mystic Henry Vaughan, opening a poem titled "The World." "I heard a fly buzz when I died," said Emily Dickinson. "So much depends upon a red wheelbarrow," said William Carlos Williams. And in response, we either say "all right, we'll go in with you for a moment or two, even though we have no idea what you are talking about"; or we stay outside with our feet on the ground and our head in our hands. Stories do this too. "Call me Ishmael," says the narrator at the beginning of *Moby Dick*. And either we go to sea in a strange ship with a mad captain or we stay home, resisting our imaginations and drinking coffee named after its sensible first mate, a fellow named Starbuck (who tried to persuade Ahab to go after a lot of little whales rather than one big one. Safer, he said, and a better investment of time and money). Such statements, whether in poetry or prose, present us with a fundamental challenge of faith. Either we accept them, if only for a moment . . . or else we turn around and go about our business. The word |*garube* signals the beginning of stories told by Khoekhoe hunters and herders in the Kalahari. It means "the happening that is not happening." "Once upon a time," we say . . . meaning "right now." John Keats once said that the quality of a great poet like Shakespeare was his

|Una Rooi of the ≠Khomani people singing in the land on her first visit back to the ≠Khomani's aboriginal homeland in the Kalahari. (PHOTO: J. EDWARD CHAMBERLIN)

ability to maintain opposite ideas in the mind without an irritable reaching after fact and reason. We are much more Shakespearean than we think. I often encounter students who say they don't like poetry. I remind them that they have long since passed that hurdle, knowing the lyrics of a hundred incomprehensible songs by heart.

Believing and unbelieving in this way may be natural to humans, but its ceremonies — its forms of expression — are learned, after which they become customary. This learning how to believe and not believe at the same time happens early in our lives, with the nursery rhymes and bedtime stories that are a staple of childhood in all cultures; and they constitute our first covenant in wonder with the world.

In church and mosque and synagogue and sweat lodge, the litanies of faith have a lot in common with those of literature. In court, a trial is a ceremony of belief as much as it is a chronicle of events; and the whole community is involved. Is so-and-so really innocent? Probably not, we may think. But we agree to believe the verdict, the veritable word, even though we "know" better. Is old man Bolton still alive? Probably not, but "probably" takes hold of us around that campfire as surely as the decision does in court, and often for just about as long. That's the way with belief. I believe that the earth is round; but at the same time I know that I'm standing right side up . . . which I might not be if the earth really were round. Which it is.

There is another tension in the telling of tales. It has to do with whether stories — and laws — are descriptive or prescriptive, whether they describe what has or might have happened or pre-scribe what will or ought to happen. This distinction is mirrored in the difference between what we call "natural laws," which are self-enforcing, and "positive laws" — posited or proposed by humans — whose sanction, in Edmund Burke's words, must be reason and judgment rather than will or desire. Science has become skilled at finessing these distinctions, but they are there in all storytelling, in all cultures. Covenants and constitutions are caught up here, and one reason why Robert Frost's poem has such a hold on us is be-cause of the phrase "promises to keep." Looking backward in order to go forward.

Nora Marks and Richard Dauenhauer, the Tlingit elder and comparative literary scholar who have done so much to illuminate the oral traditions of the West Coast from their home in Alaska, talk about the Tlingit word *shuka*, which defines the conditions for story-telling in that culture. Superficially, *shuka* translates as "ancestor," but when Tlingit people say "we don't know our *shuka*," they mean

Moon Mask from the Salish people of the Pacific Northwest coast.
These masks were an integral part of the stories told through the
dance dramas, especially during the winter festivals.
(PHOTO: RONALD B. HATCH)

we don't know our future, so it's clear that the English word ances-
tor is only a beginning. In fact, *shuka* turns in two directions, both
spatial and temporal, but before we get all misty-eyed about Abor-
iginal mysteries, the Dauenhauers remind us that we have English
words that do this too, words like "ahead" and "before," which can
refer both to things in the past that have gone before us or ahead of
us, and things that lie ahead of us or before us in the future . . . as
in, "she walks before me" and "it happened the day before yester-
day." There is lots more to say about *shuka* — among other things,
it refers to images or heraldic designs that give performances their
credibility, their covenant — but it is enough to know that *shuka*
comes to rest somewhere in that domain between here and nowhere,
"once upon a time" and "right now," where all stories take place.
There is no earlier or later in the Torah, say scholars as well as poets.

The phrase "a still small voice," which I used to describe the child's question to the camp counsellor — "is Old Man Bolton still alive?" — comes from a story told in the first book of Kings about Elijah and his encounter with God, or more precisely with the word of God, on Horeb, the legendary mountain of gods; and about the forsaking of the biblical covenant by his people. A question — "what doest thou here?" — is put to Elijah twice, first it seems by the Lord and then by someone — or something — else; and Elijah answers almost exactly the same way each time. "The children of Israel have forsaken thy covenant," he says, followed by his self-serving "I, even I only, am left." Here is how the passage continues:

> And, behold, the Lord passed by, and a great and strong wind rent the mountains, and brake in pieces the rocks before the Lord; but the Lord was not in the wind; and after the wind an earthquake; but the Lord was not in the earthquake; and after the earthquake a fire; but the Lord was not in the fire; and after the fire a still small voice.

Although Talmudic scholars sometimes render this last phrase as "soundless stillness," literary critic Stephen Prickett reminds us that it may be translated from Hebrew into English as "a voice of thin silence"; and the King James translation catches that contradiction, for "small" often meant "thin" in the Elizabethan speech of the time. It is a voice "as silent as light," in the words of the hymn "Immortal, Invisible, God Only Wise." The anthropologist Bronislaw Malinowski, in a book on magic, coined the phrase "weirdness coefficient" as a measure of magical power; and whatever happened to Elijah on Mount Horeb, and whoever's was that voice, it was weird . . . its weirdness intensified, as it almost always is, by our uncertainty about whether anything at all happened — remember the Khoekhoe storyline, the "happening that is not happening" — and if so, whether it happened as described. "Probably not," says the camp counsellor. But the child in us is not convinced; and like Elijah, and the children round the campfire, we are filled with dread.

At the centre of Elijah's story is that forsaken covenant, and accompanying it a change in the weather. The breaking of the word, and the break up of the world. Are they — or *how* are they — related? Are the wind and the rock slide and the earthquake and the fire connected to the covenant? Even Elijah doesn't seem sure; and he is a prophet, presumably better at this than the rest of us. The one thing he *is* sure of is that he is in the presence of forces beyond his understanding, and beyond his control. But are these forces natural, or supernatural? And is there any difference?

Volcanoes and earthquakes and wind storms have often appealed to both religious and scientific imaginations. The British historian R.J. White once described how, after two earthquakes devastated Lisbon in the 1750s, people began to think they were being punished for some terrible wrong they had done. One such cataclysm might be geological, he wrote; two or more were definitely theological. The coastal village of Port Royal in my second home, Jamaica, was laid waste by an earthquake in 1692 which left the few buildings still standing at a crazy angle and the landscape all but upside down. It was once known as "the wickedest city in the world" because it harboured pirates and privateers — the entrepreneurs of the old global economy, buccaneers with government backing — and many thought the Port Royal earthquake was divine retribution. "There never happens an earthquake," said the Boston Puritan Cotton Mather about the Port Royal cataclysm, "but God speaks to men on Earth."

A little later, scientists took up the story. There was a devastating earthquake at Concepción in Chile in 1835, and at the time some thought it had been caused by an Amerindian witch who had been so insulted by the people that she went up into the mountains and plugged the volcanoes. When Charles Darwin visited Concepción just after the quake, the wide-ranging speculation surrounding it influenced his thinking about the origin of both islands — he had begun his career as a geologist — and of species. To Robert FitzRoy, the Captain of HMS *Beagle* on which Darwin travelled, the explanation was theological. The earthquake was an "act of God," a language and a logic still used in the law of contracts. But FitzRoy had also given Darwin the copy of Charles Lyell's recently published *Principles of Geology* that he took along with him on the journey (which lasted from 1831 to 1836); and Lyell was the prophet of modern geology, to whom Darwin dedicated his own *Journal* of his voyage on the Beagle. To Lyell, and to Darwin, the cause was a break in the crust of the earth caused by fire and molten rock down below.

Which made it no less wonderful, for wonder comes in various guises and does not always fall neatly into scientific or religious categories. "Sooner or later every valley shall be exalted, and every mountain and hill shall be made low, and the crooked shall be made straight," said Isaiah. So did Charles Lyell. When Darwin returned from his voyage his first writings were on the geology of the places he had visited — *The Origin of Species* was published twenty years later. But he referred in his notes to what he called the "pleasure of the imagination" that his experiences gave him, admitting that even after all his geological speculations he still had an "ill-defined notion of land covered with ocean, former animals, slow force cracking surface." It was, he concluded, all "truly poetical."

Neither prophets nor scientists have all the answers, but poets sometimes have the questions, and there is an echo of Elijah's strange encounter in a poem by William Wordsworth, written after he had met an old leech gatherer on the moor. He described him as "like a Sea-beast crawled forth, that on a shelf / Of rock or sand reposeth" — a creature from the natural world, or maybe the black lagoon — and twice he asks him "how is it that you live, and what is it you do?" Twice Wordsworth is answered in "choice word and measured phrase, above the reach / Of ordinary men; a stately speech; / Such as grave livers do in Scotland use, / Religious men, who give to God and Man their dues." Which was to say, the leech gatherer spoke like a Scots Covenanter, keeping the faith; but even though he speaks clearly, Wordsworth cannot seem to understand what he is saying. And yet he recognizes in his encounter something else, something beyond words. A covenant in wonder.

William Wordsworth
(1770–1850)

Wordsworth also wrote about songs that leave us wondering, listening to "The Solitary Reaper"; and in "London, 1802" he praises John Milton's voice, "whose sound was like the sea." Not exactly the language of clarity. And yet it is clearly the language of poetry. In "The Idea of Order at Key West" Wallace Stevens picks up the theme, describing a woman singing a song by the seashore. "She sang beyond the genius of the sea," it begins:

> It was her voice that made
> The sky acutest at its vanishing.
> She measured to the hour its solitude.
> She was the single artificer of the world
> In which she sang.

Here is the voice of authority, the voice of a singer who makes — or makes up — the world, the single artificer of the world in which she sang. A trickster too:

> The song and water were not medleyed sound
> Even if what she sang was what she heard,
> Since what she sang was uttered word by word.

She sings in a tradition founded on a covenant between words and the world, between letter and spirit, between maker and diviner. Which leads to the question of the poem:

> For she was the maker of the song she sang.
> The ever-hooded, tragic-gestured sea
> Was merely a place by which she walked to sing.
> Whose spirit is this? we said, because we knew
> It was the spirit that we sought and knew
> That we should ask this often as she sang.

*Wallace Stevens
(1879–1955)*

Whose spirit is this? Whose is the still, small voice we hear after the earthquake and the fire, or what Stevens calls "the grinding water and the gasping wind," the voice that underwrites meaning and value? It is no accident that the messenger in the Greek pantheon was the trickster Hermes, and that Biblical and literary interpretation take his name in hermeneutics, where there is no interpretation without belief and no belief without interpretation. It is a circular deal we've made with our singers and storytellers and the scholars that celebrate them.

At the end of Stevens' poem the speaker turns to a companion, for like many modern poems (such as Robert Browning's "My Last Duchess" and T.S. Eliot's "Love Song of J. Alfred Prufrock") and ancient ones (like Elijah's) this is a dramatic monologue:

> Ramon Fernandez, tell me, if you know,
> Why, when the singing ended and we turned
> Toward the town, tell why the glassy lights,
> The lights in the fishing boats at anchor there,
> As the night descended, tilting in the air,
> Mastered the night and portioned out the sea,
> Fixing emblazoned zones and fiery poles,
> Arranging, deepening, enchanting night.
>
> Oh! Blessed rage for order, pale Ramon,
> The maker's rage to order words of the sea,
> Words of the fragrant portals, dimly-starred,
> And of ourselves and of our origins,
> In ghostlier demarcations, keener sounds.

Blessed rage for order. William Blake called it "fearful symmetry," adding the word "dread" to underline the fearfulness with which he (like Elijah and dreadlocked Rastafarians) contemplates Jah, while

Stevens conjured up "the maker's rage" and ghostly demarcations . . . and a mysterious pale companion. Asked who Ramon Fernandez was, Stevens said he was just anyone, a Spanish John Doe in Key West. But it turns out that he was also a French formalist critic whose work Stevens knew very well. So form and order, blessed form and spiritual order, sustain belief in this song. Forms are the food of faith, said Oscar Wilde. Northrop Frye — who was deeply influenced by Wilde, though he seldom acknowledged it — insisted in an essay on "Design as a Creative Principle" that form is much more likely to hold an audience than content. We believe in form; and the arts show us what Stevens called the "sudden rightness" of certain forms, forms whose ultimate appeal is in wonder, in mystery and enchantment, the night sky and the campfire, in ceremonies of belief in which the words have to be right, and where what the poet Thom Gunn called "the dull thunder of approximate words" will smudge the form and break the spell.

Which is why discipline is required in the language of the arts and the sciences, in the litany of religious faiths and in the legislation of governments. Listen to Confucius, teaching 2500 years ago and recorded in his *Analects*:

> If names be incorrect, speech will not follow its natural sequence. If speech does not follow its natural sequence, nothing can be established. If nothing can be established, no rules of conduct or music will prevail. Where rules of conduct and music do not prevail, law and punishments will not be just. When law and punishment are not just, the people will not know where to place their hands and feet.

Just so, a ceremony of belief works only if it is correctly performed, though we cherish the illusion that it all comes naturally. The poet struggles through countless drafts to make his poem seem spontaneous. The pianist works night and day to play the piano properly. When we try to explain this, we often end up blubbering like J. Alfred Prufrock: "That is not it at all. / That is not what I meant, at all." And then, running out of the right words, we retreat with

Prufrock into a moment of wonder, walking along the beach and listening to the mermaids singing to each other. The composer and pianist Robert Schumann was once asked to explain a particularly difficult piece of music he had written. He played it again.

In a series of radio broadcasts for the CBC *Ideas* program that had just been started in the mid-1960s by Phyllis Webb and William Young, the poet Earle Birney turned to Confucius for a list of the reasons for reading and listening to stories and songs. A couple of them are nicely contradictory: they bring us nearer to community, preserving traditional values; and they foster uprising against oppression, teaching us to stand apart. Then he added several others. Stories and songs, he said, "help us to remember the names of birds, animals, plants, trees; and they make us aware of things, and sharpen our vision." In Birney's words, they help us "spot that bird, as well as name it." David Livingston Yali-Manisi, a contemporary !Xhosa praise singer or *imbongi*, was once asked how he prepares for an impromptu performance. "*Imbongi* is eyes," he said. "He watches." Seeing, and naming. And remembering. Mnemosyne, the muse of Memory in the Greek pantheon, has always been the patron saint of poetry. But she also gives us our surest sense of home, of who we are and where we belong. The Native American writer Sherman Alexie has a poem titled "Spokane, 1976" which speaks of this:

> Once, my father saw an old Indian
> man weeping on the corner and drove around the block
>   twelve times
> before he remembered the old man's name
> and shouted it out the window so the old man would also
>   remember.

No one who has read Patrick Lane's magnificent memoir, *There Is A Season*, would doubt that your life sometimes depends upon getting the words right, on the scrupulous naming of things without evasion or equivocation — the birds and insects and flowers and the incorrigible English ivy of his garden, as well as the vodka and the violence and the fatal memories of his family.

‡Khomani children listening to a traditional storyteller in the Kalahari.
(PHOTO: J. EDWARD CHAMBERLIN)

"The best words in the best order" was Coleridge's definition of poetry, though like Stevens with his sudden rightnesses, he didn't say how to recognize what's best, or what's right. Tom Wayman, whose critical writings deserve more attention than they get, quotes the California Beat poet Lew Welsh on how a revelation can turn on unlikely words:

> Once, on the way to Oregon, I stopped at a California winery to get free wine from the tasting room. Just at that time a tour was starting so I decided to go along. A young man of about 23 was the guide and began that strange kind of language guides use, almost a chant . . . and on the left a 1,500 gallon redwood barrel containing Burgundy kept always at the temperature of . . . and then he said "Whose kid is that?"
>
> The force of "whose kid is that" caused everyone to pay attention to the real moment we were all in. A small child was about to fall into a very deep vat of wine.

"I vowed, at that moment," said Welsh, "that every statement in my poem should have at least the force of "whose kid is that?" It is an impossible standard, but a good one," he continued:

Few really bad lines can stand against it. The guide in the winery, at the moment he said "whose kid is that?," was using language in an exact relationship with his consciousness. He was trying to get some work done . . . and the people responded immediately. The child, thereby, was saved. Poetry should be at least as intense as this. It very seldom is. The few poems we prize over the centuries are.

And they all meet the test of wonder. Believable forms — like best words and sudden rightnesses — vary across cultures; but moments of wonder are universal. We read a good poem or listen to a fine song over and over again not to figure out what it means but to get another fix on beauty and truth and goodness, another covenant in wonder. It is not abstract ideals but realities of custom, traditions of form, that establish the credibility of these covenants, *underwriting* them. Wallace Stevens knew all about underwriting; he was a lawyer, and for over twenty years the vice-president of Hartford Accident and Indemnity Insurance Company (latterly known as The Hartford Financial Group).

Stories and songs are underwritten by ceremonies of belief that engage us as individuals, often only for a moment. Religious creeds and national anthems, on the other hand, require collective assent, a saying or a singing together in a congregational moment of wonder. It, too, usually lasts only as long as the occasion itself, but in such moments we believe. We go beyond "probably" to "yes."

That was the burden of John Henry Newman's *Grammar of Assent*, one of the great Victorian statements of faith, in which he entertained the question of whether we can believe what we cannot understand. "Yes" was his answer. Yet just as many languages have no single word for yes or no but embed the positive or negative in their grammar, Newman realized that there was no word for the "yes" he was looking for outside the grammar of creeds and canticles and covenants and the language of the liturgy, the ceremonies that generate wonder.

Edmund Burke once said that we are "by our constitution religious animals." Saying yes — believing — seems to come more easily to us than saying no. We want to believe. We need to believe. We are all covenanters, deal-makers, promise keepers. Scientists know this, which is why they keep making up good stories and changing them when belief starts slipping away. All over the world, people believe; and they get very impatient with unbelievers, or with those who question their beliefs, whatever they are. Somewhere down deep, people realize that the unbelievers are questioning the deal they have made, whether in their religious convictions, their social commitments, or their scientific conclusions.

Newman might also have agreed that we believe out of habit. In the Middle Ages, when you learned a language, it was said that you had the "habit" of it (from the Latin *habitus*, itself a translation of the Greek word *hexis*, referring to the essence of something). Just as we get into the habit of a language, so we get into the habit of belief. In the case of a language, we learn its words, and its grammar; and if we learn them early, we forget the learning and assume it all comes naturally. But it doesn't. A child learns that C-A-T is both a cat and nothing but an arbitrary set of sounds and (later) of letters, and then she learns about the contradictions of songs and stories, how they are both true and not true all at the same time. After that, believing them becomes a habit.

The same applies to learning the material words and grammar of the place where we live, its geology and geography, its flora and fauna, its essential character. As with language, if we learn this early we forget about the learning. But those who have recently moved to Canada, or to a new part of Canada, like those who have recently learned a new language, will know about this, just as indigenous peoples know how strangely the rest of us think and feel and behave in this — for us — new world, with our imported languages. A few years ago, the Barbadian writer Kamau Brathwaite got a lot of press and made himself very popular in postcolonial circles for lamenting that the hurricanes which are part of his Caribbean world do not howl in the rhythms of English verse. But this kind of thing could be said about every literary form that has not acclimatized itself. David Wagoner, a poet from Washington state on the Pacific coast, tells of coming over the Cascade Mountains and down into the coast rainforest for the first time in the fall of 1954. "It was a big event for me," he writes. "It was a real crossing of a threshold, a real change of consciousness. Nothing was ever the same again." This feeling is familiar to all of us, I suspect, and prompts the question of whether differences between places are like differences between languages, creating distinct ways of being in the world. Although I would not want to discount such a question, in an important sense the answer doesn't matter. What matters is that the idea of a covenant in wonder *is* the same in each place, and in every language. "Language listens to the world, I listen with it. What I hear is a question, which is listening itself," writes Robert Bringhurst in *The Tree of Meaning.*

Wagoner used the image of crossing a threshold to describe his felt change of consciousness, an image we also meet in the language of "entering" into a covenant. "Taking" treaty was a phrasing common in the 19th century, with deliberately sacramental associations. The openings of stories and songs represent another kind of invitation to enter; and T.S. Eliot used the image in the title of his early collection of essays, *The Sacred Wood*, which included his well-known "Tradition and the Individual Talent." For him, talent had no meaning outside the tradition, which is to say outside the sacred wood, just as God had no meaning outside the covenant in Elijah's story. On the same principle, the decorative flourishes of treaties between Aboriginal peoples and settler societies need to be interpreted according to the traditions within which they came into being, traditions which underwrite them, and which — to the bewilderment of some folks — often fuse or confuse the protocols of each. They are as much about places as they are about peoples, both peoples. And they presume the fundamental truth about covenants: if the deal is broken, then place and people are without meaning or value. Belief in both is gone.

The idea of a sacred space in which ceremonies of belief take place is familiar from classical times, which is where Eliot got it. Theatre provides a secular example of such a space, which may explain why theatrical drama travels so well across cultures. When we cross the threshold and enter a theatre — including a lecture theatre — we come into another world, a world in which reality is transformed by our imaginations. The same happens when we enter a church or a synagogue or a mosque or the circle of a sweetgrass ceremony. We cross a threshold when we enter the ceremonies of science too. I don't just mean the physical threshold of a laboratory, that place set apart for scientific experiments, but the imaginative threshold — the theatre of inquiry — that is signalled when a scientist says "let us imagine" something: the model of an atom, for example; or the movement of light; or the long march of evolution. Nobody has ever actually seen these things; and yet everyone believes in them, as least for the duration of the scientific ceremony — the theories of science constitute these ceremonies — just as we believe what is happening in church or mosque when the gospels are being read or the Qur'an recited, or in a theatre while a movie or a play is going on . . . and then walk outside into a world where not everyone looks like Brad Pitt and Angelina Jolie and not everyone behaves like Hamlet and Ophelia. Or we return to real life where atoms are out of sight, and light is just light — neither a wave nor a particle but something that lets us look around — and where evolution is a long-term theory rather than a short-term practice. But if *that* is reality, what was going on in the theatre, when we were laughing and crying and frozen with fear and delirious with delight? Or in church or mosque when we were filled with amazing grace. Or when all the elements of the atom were displayed to us in an ingenious diagram and the story of natural selection made good sense. And what is it that happens when the mathematician says "let x be one axis and y the other and r the radius, and then $x^2 + y^2 = r^2$ is a circle" . . . a real circle, *every* real circle you can imagine? Dear gorgeous nonsense? Yes and no.

Of course, the theatre experience can be — indeed in some

sense it must be — quite strange, a happening that is not happening. Perhaps this is why storytelling traditions usually signal the exit as well as the entrance to the imaginative place that I am calling the theatre. "I disappear," say !Xhosa *imbongi* at the end of their praise songs. "Jack Mandora, mih na choose none," say Jamaicans — it translates roughly as "it may be true, it may not, but whatever the case I'm out of here." Q.E.D. — *quod erat demonstrandum* — mathematicians say. "Amen," people say at the end of a prayer. All traditions of story and song have their own protocols for entering the theatre, as we have seen. It may be as simple as sitting down, picking up a book and opening it. Edgard Sienaert, scholar of oral traditions, describes how a speaker will address an audience in southern Africa, where he lives, with the Zulu greeting *Sanibonani*; and the audience will answer: *Sawubona*. Singular and plural, they mean: "I see you," and "we see you back"; and before we dismiss this as an exotic flourish we should recognize that this is very similar to the call and response greeting of school teachers and their classes. "Good morning, class." "Good morning, teacher."

It's our choice, our deal to enter into. If we want to tell Ishmael at the beginning of *Moby Dick* that we don't listen to weird men with funny names, or quibble about whether a person can really talk to us about what happened when they died, or dismiss that red wheelbarrow as something upon which nothing at all depends except Old Macdonald's manure, or give the teacher the finger, then we can do so. But we will pay a price, because we will be held in thrall by reality alone; and reality can make John Keats's "la belle dame" seem merciful. For the world has a way of insisting on itself, of compelling us to accept the terms of its temporary categories, of hypnotizing us into the delusion that its elements are permanent, its priorities immutable. When we submit to that world by accepting its demands, we move closer and closer to what Henry David Thoreau once described as a life of quiet desperation, in which we are always under pressure to react to what is happening outside ourselves, or elsewhere. That's if we are lucky. If we are unlucky, we become violent, or go mad. Or we surrender to the first thing that offers us survival of any sort, or any sort of power. It is only through the pressure of the imagination that we can resist this overwhelming pressure of reality. In this sense, *all* stories — from the sciences as well as from the arts — are resistance stories. They give us a way of creating a centre of belief — which paradoxically involves a different kind of surrender — from which we can move out to live in the world of events.

Such stories represent the tradition of words and images in the sciences and the arts that constitute our cultures. Different cultures, of course, and therefore different stories, not all of which we can accommodate at the same time; that seems to be an awkward fact. But if we teach one properly, our respect for others should follow. From time immemorial, stories and songs — along with paintings and carvings and dancing and music, in caves and cathedrals and longhouses and teepees — have been our first line of defence against both the threats of the everyday and the terrors of the unknown.

The unknown, and uncertainty, rule in the world of story and song; and wonder is their presiding spirit. Within the confidence of our disciplines and the storylines they promote, we sometimes forget about the importance of uncertainty, and how recently many of our contemporary certainties have been achieved. So let me sing a short praise song to uncertainty. It's in the language of seafaring, which we still use when we navigate the internet and surf the web, so those uncertainties are closer than we think. When I began sailing on the west coast, the nautical charts of the Pacific — the Admiralty charts — were filled with so-called "islands" marked P.D. and E.D. The first meant "position doubtful"; and the second, "existence doubtful." This was the 1950s, not the 1590s; and it was not encouraging. But it did keep us watching, and wondering; and in that way it kept us safe by ensuring that we navigated on the assumption that we were always almost lost. Good navigators habitually make this assumption, as the East Coast writer Robert Finley reminds us, which is one of the reasons why they use storytelling language when they "plot" their position on a chart . . . in pencil, because such a plotline is always in draft.

The feeling of being lost is still very much part of all our experience. It's not all bad, and it has a history that goes back well before modern times. The word disoriented, which we often use to describe how we feel when we're not sure where we are, was first coined centuries ago to describe what it was like to venture far from a centre of certainties. For the medieval Christian and Jewish and Islamic sailors who went out from the Mediterranean onto the Atlantic ocean, that centre was in the east — the Orient — where they identified their spiritual as well as their secular home. If they ventured too far into the western sea it was said that they would become "*dis*-oriented," alienated from their home. Portuguese sailors, who tested their limits sailing south into the then unknown, came up with a similar word to describe how they felt when they were far from their northern home, and the north star by which they navigated. They said they were *desnoreados*. Dis-northered. Like disoriented, *desnoreados* still has currency as a synonym for . . . well, for being, in Finley's fine phrase, "at sea." Before satellite technology gave us GPS, being at sea meant being in a place where nothing was sure because everything was moving — the boat, the wind, the waves, the current, the tide, the stars; and where surprises were always waiting in the fog.

Being disoriented has negative connotations for us; but on the positive side it is nothing more — nor less — than not being sure about things, and being surprised by new things. Wonder, and wondering. The German language helps us here, with its two words for disorientation, or alienation: *verfremdung*, the good kind; and *entfremdung*, the bad. The good kind is what I am talking about; and in literary studies we praise it, calling it defamiliarization, or distancing, or making strange. It's what any good story does. It has its dangers, of course, but they are the dangers of being lost in a book. It is as important in the sciences as in the arts; and these days, it seems, it is even more important in commerce and finance and law and medicine. It inspires intelligent inquiry and imaginative innovation. And it keeps us humble.

Stories and songs nourish this humility, this uncertainty, even as they encourage the absolutes of truth and beauty and goodness. It is their invitation both to believe and not to believe that gives them universal appeal. Songs and stories also provide a way of coming together in ceremonies of belief that free us from the prison houses of our separate languages — and of language itself — into the company of all those who watch and listen and wonder and bear witness. The ceremonies of science, or business, or religion, or politics, or the arts — each with their own procedures and protocols — draw our attention to differences and then show us how to ignore them. They give us a way of saying "I believe" when we are not sure, of embracing every word when the words do not make sense. They build up and break down our sense of who we are and where we belong. They take place in moments of grace and they keep us in a state of wonder, so that the categories of reality and the imagination become as arbitrary as the categories of Them and Us.

But still there's that covenant. Paul Celan, the Romanian-Jewish-German poet, said that there was no difference between a handshake and a poem. It's a fine image, brought to my attention by Scott Marentette. Both handshakes and poems are binding, and both hold us together in a compact, sometimes friendly, sometimes fabulous, sometimes fatal. They seal a deal . . . which suggests that we may never actually leave the theatre of the imagination that I mentioned a moment ago. Or that wherever we go, we wonder as we wander.

Sometimes this handshake — this poem — represents a very big deal, as in the covenants with the creator that bring a people into being, and the constitutions that keep them together and others apart. The Old Testament reminds us of how this works — if Israel will be his people, Yahweh will be their God. The first words of the first of the Psalms lay down the law, a positive law that in the covenant becomes a natural law: the godly "shall be like a tree planted by the rivers of water . . ." while the ungodly "are like the chaff which the wind driveth away." This is Them and Us writ large.

Literary traditions, being testimonial, are also covenantal, though at first glance not so dramatically. But since they begin with language, by means of which people establish their individual, collective and often national identity, they have a greater role than we may recognize. Indeed, so important is our sense of being included in this literary deal that we become convinced that a community doesn't amount to much if it doesn't have a literature, variously defined, and we can see this conviction at work in the ambition of groups within a society to have their own literature, whence women's literature, or queer literature, or black literature. In this scenario, you are either in or out of the deal by virtue of being part of the group or not; one of Us, or one of Them.

Do we choose this, or are we chosen? This question frames the two ways in which we define individual identity: by blood, over which we have no control; or by allegiance, which we choose. In turn, this generates two concepts of community: on the one hand as an *organic* entity to which we belong, willy nilly (like our family, which we imagine as a tree with branches); and on the other as an *organized* group which we build (like a neighborhood, or a nation). Together, like warp and woof, these two models influence the way we weave together our consciousness of individual self with our surrender to a sense of community. This fabric extends to our embrace of stories and songs, and Eliot's sense of a literary tradition, though covenantal in character was cosmopolitan in effect, for it presumed constants in human affairs across time and space.

I said that humans are hard-wired for belief; and more, that we are a deal-making species, bound by the words and the grammar, the habits and the ceremonies, that surround and sustain these deals. In the opening chapter of his book *God's Peoples*, the historian Donald Akenson describes the covenantal belief of South African Boers, Israeli Jews and Ulster Scots and their conviction that they must remain separate from, and superior to the non-covenantal peoples among whom they inevitably live. The idea of a divine deal between certain people and their creator generates the belief that they have been chosen to live right there, with promises to keep. Furthermore, neither the god nor the people nor the place have any identity outside such covenants, and it is therefore crucial not just to maintain belief but to defend it against unbelievers.

Let me quote a passage about an alternative in which difference has been eliminated and covenantal deals have been discredited. This is world shaped by consolidated values and a belief in global custom, where

> all old-established national industries have been destroyed . . . dislodged by new industries, whose . . . products are consumed not only at home but in every corner of the globe. In place of the old wants, satisfied by the production of the country, we find new wants, requiring for their satisfaction the products of distant lands and climes. In place of the old local and national seclusion and self-sufficiency, we have intercourse in every direction, universal inter-dependence of nations. As in material, so also in intellectual production. The intellectual creations of individual nations become common property. National one-sidedness and narrow-mindedness become more and more impossible, and from the numerous national local literatures there arises a world literature.

Sounds good? This is Karl Marx and Friedrich Engels, in the covenant they called *The Communist Manifesto*, describing a world in which the bourgeoisie has transformed the world. It is a world in which diversity is replaced by commonality, where national literatures, national languages, and the covenants and constitutions that underwrite them are no longer. It has a familiar feel to it, this world, especially in parts of the academy where "world literature" holds sway. And it makes many of us very uneasy.

But the alternative has its own unsettling consequences, and I don't just mean — to pick up Donald Akenson's triad — the politics of South African apartheid, the Israeli siege mentality, the Northern Irish civil war — though they are certainly part of the picture. But we are *all* part of the picture; and a country like Canada, which rightly privileges the choices people make to come here and make this their home, has to find a way of accepting — no, more than that, of *believing* — that at the centre of our country are the Aboriginal peoples who believe *they* were chosen to be where they are — or sadly, for many of them, where they once were and from where they are now exiled — because of their covenant with their creator. Like all covenanters, they have promises to keep and unbelievers to keep out. Their defining deal is not with the Crown, but with their Creator.

This is both a contemporary and an uncomfortable fact. For those who see themselves as chosen people, as Akenson points out, their covenant is not a code to be deciphered — here he is recalling Northrop Frye and the title of his book on the Bible, *The Great Code* — but a code that determines their destiny, the way a genetic code does. Sometimes they believe they have been chosen to suffer; always, that they are bound to return. Both in a binding covenant. As Akenson suggests in the last lines of his book,

> the Hebrew covenantal structure has lasted from the middle bronze age to the present. It is one of the few things in human society that we can take for granted in the sense that it will be here longer than we will. Indeed, much longer. Modern-day Israel is only the most recent society to conform to the covenantal blueprint, but it will not be the last. Others will follow, for the covenant, as found in the books of Moses, is particularly suited to the sorts of smaller societies that are inevitably produced as great empires come apart and as small ethnic groups become independent of their former masters. Far from disappearing . . . the covenantal cosmology, based on the ancient Hebrew template, will be one of the most effective ways for a myriad of small nations to fortify themselves in a world that will increasingly be confusion and whirl.

Is this a genial prospect? Like the camp counsellor, I'd say "probably not." But also like him, I've got another story at hand.

One of the disadvantages — the only one, I should quickly add — of being married to the poet Lorna Goodison is that I cannot write about her poetry as often as I used to. But I can quote it. The following poem is called "Heartease," and its association with covenants and catechisms will be obvious, along with its confusion of Pentecostal and planetary fire, celestial vexation and an earthly vision of peace, the Qur'an and the Bible, the Old Testament and the New.

In what looked like the blackout last week
a meteorite burst from the breast of the sky
smoking like a censer, it spelled out in
incandescent calligraphy
a message for all who had deep eyes.

If you did not see I'll tell you
what it said:
cultivate the search-me-heart and
acres of sincerity grass and turn
your face towards Heartease.

Set out a wash pan and catch mercy rain
forget bout drought, catch the mercy rain,
bathe and catch a light from this meteoric flame
and sit down cleansed, to tell a rosary of your
ancestor's names.
A singing chain of ancient names to bind them tight
all who work evil downward through the night.
And toward morning the sun come and tell you
"sleep. I'll mark your place with this azure/rose ribbon
taken from the hidden locks of the dawn.
Sleep in the day and you will dream when you sleep
the second surah of this message."

And who hear, do all that and sleep in the darkened day and
dream as them sleep, how the one whose hand draw the veil,
(for it was not a blackout) the one who fling the meteor
was in a celestial vexation
saying, Imagine, how I put you here in this most favoured place
and look how you take it and less count it.
Look how you root up my rarest blooms,
look how you take my flower bed dem turn tombs,
look how you eye red from looking over a next one yard
from envying everything him have.
Like him concrete-stressed-cast-iron-lawn
and him man-made-robot-made-by-man-to-replace-man,
you want to know how far this thing gone?
Some calling Siberia a nice open land.

At this point it look like him was too grieved to go on.
Him had to drink some dew water from the throat
of a glass-petalled flower.
And when His wrath was dampened He spoke again:
I have many names and one is merciful . . .
So in that name I have decided that the veil I draw
will be lifted, when you look to the condition of
your part of this yard.
When you stop draw blood cross the promise line
in the young people's palms.
When the scribes cleanse their hands and rise
to write new psalms.
When you sight up why outta the whole human race
is you of all people I choose to dwell in this place.

So who hear send me here to tell you say
we do not know bout the intention of a next one
but we catching mercy rain in zinc and tub pan
and in addition
to the search-mi-heart
the sincerity seeds
and the pilgrimage to Heartease
we planting some one-love
undivided ever-living healing trees.
So next week if you want to come, welcome,
for we going to set up again
to extend the singing rosary of our ancestors' names
till the veil is rent from the eyes of the sky
of everyone
forever and ever
illumination.

Here are both the old and the new covenants. Here, too, are the contradictory elements of choice for a chosen people, bringing together the coercive and the compassionate dynamics of a covenant. And while covenants are by no means an exclusively Judeo-Christian inheritance, their spirit — inherited from nomadic ancestors who probably had a lot in common with Aboriginal peoples around the

Lorna Goodison
(PHOTO: DENIS VALENTINE)

world — may explain why the Bible has been so easily assimilated into many traditions. Our common ground lies in ceremonies of belief, and the wonder they occasion.

That said, it is surprisingly common to hear discrediting remarks about the oral traditions of nomadic peoples such as those whose stories and songs make up the Bible, traditions which — like all literary traditions — celebrate the dynamics of a deal. In fact, these oral traditions also mirror the covenantal character inherent in the ceremonies of churches, courts and schools, all of which depend upon a customary accord between speakers and listeners, the ceremonial equivalent of a handshake. Still, the perceived "primitive" quality of orality seems to trouble people, just as it troubled Marshall McLuhan and his student Walter Ong when they dismissed such traditions as lacking the sophistication of abstract thought, less evolved than written traditions, blurring the boundaries — to which some seem almost pathologically committed — between thought and feeling, the secular and the sacred, the material and the spiritual. Mostly, this dismissal is the result of ignorance, and an almost willful misunderstanding of oral traditions; but it is not just literary and liturgical commentators who discount them. Donald Akenson describes how in his profession of history the founding fathers have generally been classical figures such as Herodotus and Thucydides, mirroring the dominance of classical languages and literatures for millennia in the humanities. "The classics," Akenson suggests, "were, well, so much classier as intellectual antecedents than were the texts that had their origin in the oral traditions of a group of Semitic nomads from the back of beyond." These, of course, were the texts that constituted the Old Testament, the old covenant; and it is worth noting too that they gave us the understanding of history as narrative which historiographers cherish these days. They were also, of course, dependent on oral traditions.

—☙

I was thinking of such nomads a few years ago, when I was present on another occasion when a covenant was celebrated. It was a covenant in wonder, rather than in biblical wisdom; and it was, typically, only for a moment. But it happened. And it signalled a habit, like the language in which it was expressed.

It was early spring out on the steppes of central Asia where a rider was herding animals down from the hills onto the open plains as the grass turned green and the sky took on a Buddhist blue. Standing in short stirrups and riding like the wind, he swept through the herds with a dancer's grace and a gymnast's daring, watching and listening like a doctor on rounds. Having just finished a book about horses and history, I had gone riding in northeastern Mongolia — the heartland of horse cultures — with my son Geoff and a young lad

A contemporary Mongolian herder on horseback with his herd of horses.
(PHOTO: J. EDWARD CHAMBERLIN)

named Gohe from one of the nomad families. They had moved from the winter shelter of the mountains to the open prairie a month or two before, and were settling in for the summer season of calving and lambing and foaling and caring for the health of their herds. The Mongolian herder's life is hard and dangerous, easy to exoticize but difficult to describe with adequate respect for the knowledge it requires, and for the way in which it transcends material and spiritual categories. These Mongolian nomads are both dreamers and down to earth. They eat horsemeat, and drink mare's milk, and they herd horses for food and as symbols of wealth and power; but like our ancestors — who painted horses on the walls of caves forty or fifty thousand of years ago — and like our own children — who put up wall calendars of wild horses in their bedrooms — they celebrate the grace and beauty as well as the strength and stamina of horses.

One day as we were riding out on the steppes in a driving rain and fierce wind, several horses appeared on the horizon, their mood restless with the coming change in weather and the constant sense of danger that horses carry with them. Gohe stopped; and for a moment he and his horse stood there as amazed as the cowboy gazing at the stars in "Home on the Range," or any of us singing "Amazing Grace." *Takh*, he said, pointing at them. *Takh* means "spirit" in Mongolian. It is also the word for a wild horse.

Once again in Wallace Stevens' words, whose spirit? We knew it was the spirit that we sought and knew that we should ask this often. Technically, those horses on the horizon weren't wild, though the closest to a wild horse — the so-called Przewalski pony — is native to Mongolia. There are no truly wild horses anywhere anymore, though wildness is itself a ceremonial category (as Scott Russell Sanders implied when he described wilderness as a kind of Sabbath). Gohe knew all that; and seeing horses on the horizon was certainly not unusual — his family had a couple of hundred horses in their herd, and horses were everywhere out there on the steppes. But in that ceremonial moment, and for that moment, his faith in something beyond him converged with his knowledge of things around. It separated him from Geoff and me as surely as his language did. And it also bound us together.

— ☙

Covenants represent a deal, and accordingly, they often have a seal that confirms this. It may be something that signals the keeping of a promise: a rainbow, or horses on the horizon, or bread and wine, or a piece of paper; and this material component of covenants, the letter of their law, is as ancient as their spirit. I mentioned something else about covenants earlier. They and the laws they invoke are almost always poised — like the Tlingit *shuka* — between past and future, between a promise made and a promise kept, between describing and prescribing. Or between reality and the imagination, waking and dreaming.

I have in my keeping another covenantal text, in the form of a traditional horsemen's quirt, a ceremonial riding crop of Siksika (Blackfoot) heritage. It is about eighteen inches long and two inches wide in the shape of a small cricket bat; and is intricately carved with a braided leather tail about three feet long and ornamental buffalo hide bound in at the end. This quirt was in my grandfather's possession since the 1880s, when he settled in Fort Macleod in southern Alberta.

I do not know how it came into his hands, though he had close associations with the Blackfoot. It was certainly given to him, and he must have known its owner well. I have begun discussions to see whether it may have been part of a medicine bundle; and if so, it belongs back with the Blackfoot, to be opened and read again after the first thunder every spring, inspiring like a covenant and interpreted like a constitution.

In one sense, this quirt — and the story it tells — is a charm. It makes things happen in the world, and it needs to be read for its power to be realized. It is also a riddle, presenting us with a contradiction that (given the convention of riddling) we take to be true. All

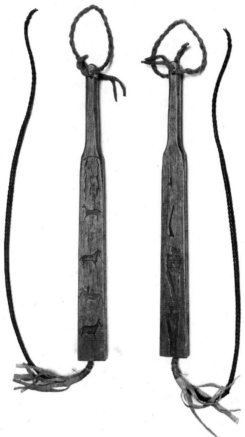

Blackfoot quirt carved by Crop-Eared Wolf and given to the author's grandfather. (PHOTO: JULIE COCHRANE)

literature and liturgy and legislation, and all scientific theories, are located somewhere on the spectrum between riddles and charms.

As part of a BBC documentary on my grandfather's life and times, I took the quirt back to the foothills a few years ago to have it read by experts, both native and non-native. My first reader was an ethnographer — a local legend named Gerald Conaty — at the Glenbow Museum in Calgary. He told the stories that he discerned from the quirt. There were three successful raids against other tribes represented by wave-like lines, as well as eight scouting and horse-

Detail of the
Blackfoot quirt.

stealing adventures. Along with a gun and a pipe, two men figure on one side of the quirt, both carved and coloured in traditional Blackfoot style; one was the owner, and the other represented all those he had killed in battle and from whom he had taken horses — his covenantal enemies.

On the other side are four horses, all finely rendered. Each of them represents horses that were stolen. Horse-stealing was very important to many of the plains tribes, part of a deliberate defiance of the categories and choices that so often interfere with our ability to understand the world. It was a form of storytelling, celebrating the virtues of thievery and trickery and the telling of tales, fellow travellers from time immemorial. For their part, the horses were both worthless and priceless, and like great art did not really "belong" to anyone but were in a kind of serial stewardship. The quirt was made when the North-West Mounted Police were trying to make horse-stealing a thing of the past. The carver of this quirt had something else in mind.

The horses are coloured differently — two are shades of yellow/gold, one is red, and the one at the bottom is blue. The Blackfoot have nearly a hundred words for the different colours of horses, but not as many colours in their palette. One remarkable thing about the horses is that two of them have reins running down to the ground. This, I learned, signified that they were particularly prized. They would have been attached by the reins at night to the ankle or wrist of the owner as he slept in his teepee, and the horse thief must have had extraordinary skill to steal them from camps in which there would be fifty or a hundred dogs at any given time. The "horse" on the bottom is especially intriguing, for its ears stand straight up; and indeed it isn't a horse at all, but a mule. Mules were new to the west at that time, brought into the region by the North-West Mounted

Police from whom this one would have been stolen. Gerry Conaty — the ethnographer — said, with disarming matter-of-factness, that the warrior must have had help stealing horses and a mule that were so highly valued and carefully watched. He and I come from the same academic background, and I thought he meant an accomplice from within the enemy camps. But he was referring to help from the spirits.

Finally, he said he had never seen a quirt quite like this one, and suggested that it might need a different kind of interpretation, one that could only be provided by elders who knew the stories — the gospel, not the gossip — surrounding one of the great chiefs of the time, Crop-Eared Wolf. For Gerry thought the quirt belonged to Crop-Eared Wolf himself, and that he would have carved it.

So I went down to a town called Stand Off, southeast of Fort Macleod, and arranged to visit an elder of the Blood (Kainai) tribe, wondering whether his account would be different. The elder, Frank Weaselhead, told stories that were precisely the same, matching in every detail Gerry Conaty's reading, including the identification of Crop-Eared Wolf as its author/carver. With one exception. He said that it was the record of a dream, not a set of real events. The story of the dream, credited to Crop-Eared Wolf, was still recalled in the tribe, he said; and it was the dream, and the carving of the covenant quirt, that brought these remarkable achievements — the raids and the horse and mule thefts — to reality. The mule had appeared to Crop-Eared Wolf to tell him that he would lead any horses he stole across the rivers in flood, when horses would typically balk. And the mule had then waited in the closely guarded North-West Mounted police encampment for Crop-Eared Wolf to come and get him. The quirt was a ceremony of belief. The events followed.

Which left me, and I leave you, with some questions. "Fled is that music. Do I wake or sleep?" asked the poet John Keats at the end of his "Ode to a Nightingale." Was this a dream carved on the quirt, preceding and predicting and prescribing the reality? Or was it a record, a description, of an extraordinary reality, still celebrated in Blackfoot territory? And what exactly is the difference anyway? Did

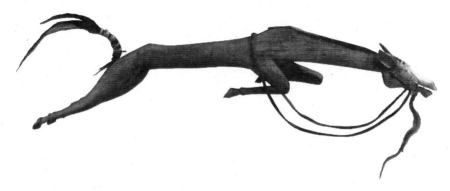

The Lakota Sioux Horse Effigy — created to honour a warrior horse that fell in battle. (PHOTO: MUSEUM OF SOUTH DAKOTA STATE HISTORICAL SOCIETY)

it really happen to Elijah as described in the book of Kings? Or was it like one of those Khoesan stories, a happening that was not happening. The answers, I believe, are to be found in the questions themselves, as is usually the way with riddles and charms. The Chinese sage Chuang Tzu, living a little after Confucius, tells of a dream he had one night, in which he was a butterfly, happily flitting about and minding his own butterfly business in a butterfly state of mind. Then he woke up, and there he was, substantially and unquestionably Chuang Tzu. Was he Chuang Tzu who had dreamed he was a butterfly? Or was he a butterfly who was dreaming he was Chuang Tzu? Probably not.

—❧

My father sang songs, and he loved puns and the play of words. But it was my mother who told most of the stories in our family, which she would do with a kind of conspiratorial flourish that would catch us up every time. She was born in 1899, and her best friend was Margaret Williams, who became my godmother. Margaret was Métis, the granddaughter of a Cree woman and a Scotsman, the chief factor of the Hudson's Bay Company in Fort Qu'Appelle in Saskatchewan during the 1880s when Louis Riel led his people in rebellion — or uprising, as they called it — against the new Dominion of Canada. Margaret's mother was twelve or thirteen at the time; and after Riel's defeat and trial for treason (when he said he'd rather be judged bad than mad), she visited him in prison in Regina every other day until his execution. How she did so, and why, is a mystery; but she kept a journal, in which Riel — who imagined himself as the psalmist David, dashing down his enemies with words and music — would write remarks like "evening prayer gives more pleasure in heaven than all the military music played by the North-West Mounted Police outside my cell window."

Louis Riel (1844–1885)

When I knew my godmother Margaret years later, she still had her mother's journal, which she would read to me like holy scripture. Margaret had met my mother in Vancouver in the early years of the century, when they were both young girls, about the same age as Margaret's mother when she visited Louis Riel. My mother's father — my grandfather — had gone west to Fort Macleod the year before Riel's uprising, and although he represented much that Riel resented about settlement in the west, he went back to Regina to support Riel at his trial. Why *he* did so is as much a mystery as those visits by Margaret's mother, though historians confirm that many westerners felt common cause with Riel in his opposition to Ottawa. *Plus ça change.* My grandfather's first wife died in childbirth; so after he married my grandmother, he sent her back to her family in Ingersoll, Ontario, to have the baby they were expecting. But she, too, died in childbirth, a day after my mother was born; and my grandfather, probably pole-axed by grief, stayed in Macleod while my mother was raised by her aunt her mother' sister, who gave up her own engagement to take my mother into a household of maiden aunts. They lavished all their attention on her, and had a tutor come to teach her about the world as far away as, well, as Brantford.

Then, when she was twelve, my grandfather sold his ranch, moved to Vancouver, built a house, and called for his daughter. I can't even begin to imagine what it must have been like for her aunt to lose the daughter she had raised since birth; and I can hardly imagine what it must have been like for my mother, travelling three thousand miles away from the only home she'd ever known, and the only family she'd ever had, to live with a man she barely knew. But she did, and went to school (scary at the best of times) for the first time in her life.

There, she met Margaret. My mother was painfully shy, at least beyond a small circle; and Margaret, like many Métis of her generation, was painfully silent about her heritage, certainly to anyone outside that same small circle. Maybe it was the spirit of Louis Riel, or my grandfather, or those formidable maiden aunts in Ingersoll, or that little half-breed girl visiting the prison in Regina, but together, they . . . well, this is the story my mother told me.

The school they went to was housed in an old building in Vancouver, with a large upstairs room — really an attic with sloping ceilings. They would go there for tea, served every afternoon to the girls. And every morning, first thing, the girls and their teachers — about sixty, all told — would traipse up the narrow stairs for assembly and prayers.

One morning, Margaret and my mother were late; and when they got to the door at the top of the stairs it was shut. The morning hymn had begun.

> New every morning is the love
> Our wakening and uprising prove . . .

Uprising? The two girls looked at each other. Then, without saying a word, they rose up and bolted the door. They heard another line — "Fit us for perfect rest above" — and they giggled. They giggled through the announcements, and through the roll call, when they were the only ones who didn't say "here, ma'am" . . . and they were still giggling when the headmistress led the school to the door at the top of the staircase and tried to open it.

That was always the end of the story. My mother would never tell me what happened next. "Use your imagination," she'd say with a smile. In my imagination, they are still there, sitting on the staircase at Crofton House School, two giggling girls wondering what they have done, and what to do next. Like Louis Riel's uprising, theirs probably lasted only a moment, but that moment — and the wonder that filled it — became mine.

And their story, unfinished as it is, became my touchstone for all stories, which like all literature and all law, all commerce and all the healing professions, all art and all science, are *always* unfinished and uncertain, full of promises to keep . . . so we can come up with new stories and new songs, and new covenants in wonder with our world.